HEATING FOOD

David Wray

Contents

OXFORD

UNIVERSITY PRESS

Great Clarendon Street, Oxford, OX2 6DP

Oxford University Press is a department of the University of Oxford.
It furthers the University's objective of excellence in research, scholarship,
and education by publishing worldwide in

Oxford New York

Athens Auckland Bangkok Bogotá Buenos Aires Calcutta
Cape Town Chennai Dar es Salaam Delhi Florence Hong Kong Istanbul
Karachi Kuala Lumpur Madrid Melbourne Mexico City Mumbai
Nairobi Paris São Paulo Singapore Taipei Tokyo Toronto Warsaw
and associated companies in Berlin Ibadan

Oxford is a registered trade mark of Oxford University Press
in the UK and in certain other countries

A CIP record for this book is available from the British Library

ISBN 0 19 915767 7
Available in packs
Pack B Pack of Six   (one of each book)   ISBN 0 19 915771 5
Pack B Class Pack   (six of each book)   ISBN 0 19 915772 3

Printed in Hong Kong

Acknowledgements

All photography by Mark Mason.

Bread

When you heat food, it changes.
Bread changes colour.

slice of bread

toast

Toast the bread.

Eggs

raw egg

Boil the egg.

Eggs go hard.

hard boiled egg

Corn

Heat in a saucepan.

raw corn

Corn pops and gets bigger.

popcorn

Cake

cake mix

Bake the cake.

Cake rises and goes firm.

baked cake

Chocolate

Heat the chocolate.

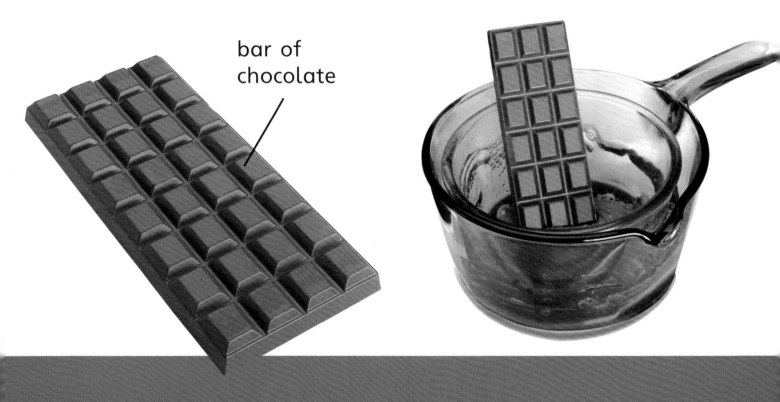

bar of
chocolate

Chocolate melts.

melted
chocolate

FACT BOX
Chocolate sets
when it gets
cold again.

Index